Courage Rises

How To Create the Life You Want
By Leaning In To Fear

SUKI JEFFREYS

All rights reserved. This book or any portion thereof may not be reproduced or used in any manner whatsoever without the express written permission of the publisher except for the use of brief quotations in a book review.

Printed in the United States of America

First Printing, 2022

ISBN: 979-8-9867474-0-8 - eBook
ISBN: 9798374913453- Print paperback

Edited By Ashly Wallace / Penning for Your Thoughts Editing

Copyright © 2022 Suki Jeffreys

To my husband, Mike Jeffreys, who has always believed in me. We are "freed and bound by our love."

CONTENTS

Foreword	i
Introduction	1
Depression	9
Moving to Australia	17
I Meet "The One"	25
Now Cancer?	35
The Thing That Scares Me the Most	49
Retirement	65
5 Ways to Lean In to Fear to Create the Life You Want	79
The 3 Roots of Fear- Limiting Beliefs, Stories, and Delusions	81
The Fear Cycle-	87
Why It's Important to Break the Cycle	90
Methods for Moving Through Fears-	93
Get Clear on Your Motivators	93
Weigh the Options	96
Just Jump In!	98
Name Your Fear	99
Tell Fear You're the Boss	101
Start Leaning In to Fear Today	104
Additional Resources	107
About The Author	109

FOREWORD

It is difficult for me to tell you how proud I am of this woman.

From the moment I met her, my spirit sensed her strength, power, love, and caring...and, I might add, the one thing that usually holds people back. Activity.

When I met her, she didn't see herself the way I did – at least not in the beginning. That's not unusual, but in true 'Suki-esque' fashion, she forged forward - She knew if she was to empower women like herself, these changes, including the acceptance of her strength, had to begin with her.

This is the value of this book. We're all on a journey, and with the guidance of these pages, you can walk along in a way that keeps each step from being scary. You'll understand that fear, in and of itself, can be defeated - one step at a time.

Through these pages, you'll see that Suki is vested. This servant leader shows you her underbelly. An "If I can do it, you can too" kind of message, walking alongside you and cheering you on with each step.

Yes, Suki exudes strength. A presence. Power, love, and caring for others. And has put herself on the line to prove it. It would best serve you to muster up the courage and pay attention to this woman if you want to push fear aside and step forward, create a legacy, or turn your long-forgotten dreams into reality.

I am privileged to call her a friend.

Donna Sparaco Meador, CWEC
International Best-Selling Author, Speaker & Co-Creator: "THE MEADOR AFFECT"

INTRODUCTION

My dad died four days before my sixth birthday. He had been fighting Osteosarcoma (bone cancer) for over a year. Before then, I don't remember feeling fear aside from a spanking after doing something wrong or getting a vaccine shot.

After that, there was a lot of fear in my life; fear of making my mom cry or doing something wrong that would make her go away. I constantly wondered if I did or didn't do something that caused my dad to go away. I was terrified of changes.

Growing up, I tried to be a people pleaser, but I wasn't very good at it. I did well in school and was very good at music.

I was opinionated, curious, and outspoken. Interested in everything, I would start projects and never finish them, leading my family to call me disorganized. I had unfinished projects everywhere.

I was excitable, and learning new things seemed fun and trendy. I was wrapped up in the idea that I *needed* to have or do something, or the world would end.

I was called shallow because I would quickly leave friends high and dry to hang out with others.

I overheard people call me bossy and scary because I tended to take charge if no one else was making decisions.

My sisters are peacekeepers, and I am not. While in high school, I wish I had a quarter for every time I heard them say, "Why can't you just shut up for once?" because I wouldn't let go of an argument. My mom would be upset about something, and I would argue her facts and opinions.

Conversely, I needed to prove my point of view. I continued this cycle again and again. I enjoy a good argument, but it was counterproductive.

I went to college in 1977 and was engaged just after graduating. In 1982, the societal expectation for women who went to college was that they would graduate, get married, get a job, and build a family.

I chose to break with that expectation, and I blew up my life by breaking off that engagement. A friend gave me a fantastic gift at that time; she said I was brave. I'd never thought of myself that way. Her sharing that with me caused me to embrace the idea slowly.

I thought about what she said quite a lot as I healed from my relationship wounds and built a new life. I decided she was right – I *was* brave! I had courage, and I learned it from my mom.

That set a strong foundation. It is not about being fearless. It is about being afraid and doing it anyway. I went into subsequent seasons of my life believing my friend and looking for more evidence that it was true.

COURAGE RISES

My newly recognized courage led me to take the following actions:

I moved across the country (Wisconsin to Southern California) at twenty-five, where I had secured a new job but had no friends.

I moved to Melbourne, Australia, at thirty, where I knew no one.

I became a traveling consultant at thirty-two, moving around the US every few months, making new friends, and building successful programs from scratch.

I defied societal norms again by breaking another marriage engagement at thirty-three.

I met and married my husband (and his three kids) at thirty-nine.

I became an entrepreneur at forty-one and realized success and fulfillment by starting an art supply business from scratch, buying my supplier, and selling it after five years.

I beat breast cancer at forty-three.

I put family first by returning to corporate life at forty-six to realize financial goals during our children's college years.

I retired from my unfulfilling corporate tech job at fifty-nine.

And I'm doing it again. Blowing up the expectations of what I "should" be doing as a sixty-three-year-old "retiree."

Even though I've had lots of travel & adventure, I still consider my life to this point as being a "corporate drone" for most of the thirty-seven years leading to my retirement.

Since then, I have developed a big dream of living happily with purpose, meaning, self-determination, health, fun, and money. Something that will propel me out of bed each morning, ready to go head-to-head with the universe!

My family and friends laugh because getting out of bed was something I only ever did under duress.

All those prior years, I went through the motions of working until retirement by working on what I *did* rather than who I *was*. I was very good at what I did, but after the last ten years, where I was in an increasingly less-satisfying role, I needed something new.

And at sixty-three, I'm not done!

Transition.

Pivot.

New season, new me.

It was time to look myself squarely in the eye and challenge myself to BE more! I am more honest, fulfilled, committed, and in command of my life. I OWN my life and don't live by habit or society's expectations.

Of course, this transition has come with its own set of fears. I'll tell you about them in the Retirement Chapter.

Since founding Courage Rises, I have studied under coaches I greatly admire. I am certified as a <u>Tell Fear You're The Boss</u> and <u>Behavioral SuperPowers</u> coach. I read many books and have done a lot of interviews with people with every day (and occasionally extraordinary) stories of courage to tell. I listened to podcasts, became a best-selling author, and pioneered the idea of the Courage Continuum.

If you are contemplating a new season in life by choice or circumstance, I'm here to tell you that you are not alone and are more courageous than you think!

You CAN do anything you set your mind to.

You CAN create a life with more joy and meaning.

You CAN live with more impact in your community and the world.

You CAN create the relationships you desire.

You CAN define and achieve for yourself.

There is no such thing as TOO LATE.

Want to learn to lean into fear so you can get what you want out of life? Here is the start! Follow me as I walk you through some of the significant moments of fear and courage in my life and the strategies that allowed me to lean into my anxiety so I could experience what life has to offer!

Let's jump in!

DEPRESSION

> "To know yourself, you must sacrifice the illusion that you already do."
> -Veronika Tugaleva

Sometimes you don't know what hit you. I experienced significant depression when I was twenty-six—the kind where you don't see any point in getting out of bed.

There were so many possible causes. My broken engagement was the chief source, I think. What would become of me now that I had interrupted the "natural flow of things"?

I piled stress on by moving to a new and very different city and starting a new job in a completely different industry. I realized, years later, that I sometimes had intense hormonal fluctuations that led to PMS. I wasn't sleeping; my brain never stopped working and worrying.

I didn't notice any warning signs myself, but in the few days leading up to my shutdown, I was irritable and quick to anger.

I felt leaden – like all my limbs were weighted, and it was too much effort to get out of bed. I didn't think about eating or drinking. I just wanted to drift down into sleep and not think ever again.

I felt nothing mattered, not me, work, friends, or family. I just wanted to sleep. There was no reason to keep living except that my family would have to deal with my suicide, and I didn't want to inconvenience them. I felt so little that I didn't think my being gone would matter.

My good friend Rhonda called my mom when I stopped showing up at work. I'm forever indebted to her.

In the early days of answering machines, we could screen our calls – the device would let you listen to a message left by the caller.

Rhonda called a few times, wondering where I was, but I didn't pick up the phone. It would take too much effort, and I didn't want to talk to anyone or to explain.

Then my mom started calling and leaving messages. That was harder to ignore. She lived about forty miles away, and she wanted me to come and visit for the weekend. She bribed me with my favorite meal, spaghetti with meat sauce, and said she wanted to see me. We could sit around. There was no big plan.

She sounded worried, and I didn't want her to worry about me. I didn't want anyone to even think about me. So, I picked up the phone when I heard her voice on the machine the fourth time.

She threatened to send my dad over to pick me up if I didn't come. I knew I wouldn't be able to ignore him knocking on my door. My roommate would let him in any way.

I got out of bed for the first time in three days and felt like I weighed a million pounds. It took a lot of effort to walk or talk, but somehow, I drove there. On the way, I remember evaluating every on and off ramp as a possible way to end it all.

I was not looking forward to the conversations I knew were coming. I was sure it would be a big waste of time.

With Mom and dad sitting on the edge of the couch staring at me, it was hard to ignore their silent plea of questions. I didn't want to talk to them, but I hoped if I told them how I felt, it would stop the questions.

They were apprehensive. My dad somehow convinced me that it could get better and that I needed to talk to a professional. I was skeptical, but he gave me a referral, and I agreed to stay at their house for a few days and see the psychologist at least once. I knew I needed help.

When I talked to the doctor, he assured me he could help. He referred me to a psychiatrist for medication, and we continued for about six weeks in talk therapy before I decided I wanted to find a woman to talk to instead.

I took the recommended medication and slowly started sleeping through the night for the first time in months. It was a miracle!

I would eventually wake up rested, and I regained my energy. I wasn't constantly obsessed with what bad things would happen tomorrow, next week, or next month or how I would never be up to the task of dealing with it. The heavy feeling lifted. Not having the constant catastrophe in my head at night was a game changer.

Thirty-seven years later, I still remember driving in L.A. after starting medication and therapy: the sun was shining, my window was open, and I thought, "this is how happy people feel."

I still feel gratitude and happiness for that day as a revelation. I was also grateful that I chose to respond to my parents and agreed to therapy and medication. Those actions changed the trajectory of my life.

At 63, I am still on that medication. I went off it when I moved to Australia because I was anxious that the Australian government would find me defective somehow if I were on that medication. Australia was (probably still is) a desirable place to live, so they were very particular about who they let in at the time. I wanted to go, and I thought I might not get a visa if they knew.

After two years, I started experiencing some depression again and restarted the meds.

I occasionally still feel I am defective in some way for needing them, thinking I should have weaned myself off them long ago. However, society is catching up to the fact that mental health has many different colors and flavors, and seeking help is healthy.

In the 2020 Olympics, held in 2021 due to the pandemic, I was so pleased to see some elite athletes, like Simone Biles, Michael Phelps, and Naomi Osaka (who backed out of Wimbledon), prioritizing their mental health over the competition.

I don't have a single word for how it made me feel, but I could empathize with needing help, and it helped me feel "normal." Like these fantastic athletes were my "homies."

If you are feeling lost and hopeless, I see and feel you. Please seek help. I am living proof that it can make all the difference. There are people to talk with.

In the USA, call, text, or chat 988, the National Suicide Hotline.

In Canada, go to https://thelifelinecanada.ca/lifeline-canada-foundation/lifeline-app/ for instructions to download the LifeLine app for Online Chat, Text, and Email Crisis Help

In Australia, if you or someone you know is in crisis and needs help now, call triple zero (000). You can also call Lifeline on 13 11 14 — 24/7/365

COURAGE RISES

MOVING TO AUSTRALIA

"Courage doesn't always roar. Sometimes courage is the little voice at the end of the day that says I'll try again tomorrow."
-Mary Ann Radmachet

When I turned thirty, I moved to Australia. There were a bunch of things happening in my life.

I had a good group of friends, was having fun, and wasn't stressed about aging like some I knew. I was looking forward to it!

But there was also nothing happening in my life. I was dating a couple of men I liked, but I couldn't see a future with one, and the other didn't want to take the next step (moving in together).

When I heard from a friend that a bank in Australia was installing the software I had worked with for the past few years, I was very interested.

I thought, why not? I'm young, unattached, and speak English. I've lived in two countries already. Why not?

I interviewed with the hiring executive and got a job offer at the end of June, 1989.

I told my friends and family, quit my job, sold my furniture and my beloved convertible, then figured out how to get the rest of my stuff packed, crated, and off to Australia.

I was going there on a work visa, but I wasn't sure if I would come back, so I took what I couldn't live without: my record collection and new voltage-convertible stereo, and sold the rest. Believe it or not, someone actually bought a bridesmaid dress I had worn at my friend Lynn's wedding eight years prior!

I said goodbye to many family members at my younger sister's wedding, which conveniently was scheduled one month before I moved.

The high lasted until I got to Sydney, one state away from my new home in Melbourne. It was a curious incident that broke my bubble of excitement.

The plane landed in Sydney, and I had the opportunity to get off and walk around before boarding the plane to my final destination. It had been a long, nine-hour flight from LAX without a break, and I was glad to be walking around and breathing different air.

We landed at around 5:30 am Sydney time. There weren't many places open in the airport to get a snack early, but I found one and grabbed an apple and some potato chips.

I sat alone at a small table not far from where some airport employees were eating. I was alarmed by their conversation. It wasn't the content. I was shocked that they were speaking English, but I could only understand about one in four words.

The fear started pouring in. What was I thinking, moving halfway around the world, not knowing anyone?

Why did I think my English was everyone's English?

How was I going to understand anything at work? I was going to be sent home the first week I was there! This was a huge mistake!

I later discovered that I heard the Australian-accented English of Italian, Spanish, and Greek immigrants. Yikes! It was a real piling-on of accents.

But Pow! That one little experience led to deep homesickness.

I had never been homesick before. I had always been up for any new adventure, knowing I could survive and thrive. I was always game to sleep at a friend's house or spend a week or two at camp.

Now I was unsure. To add to my insecurity, my ride from the airport to the city of Melbourne was late. I was standing in the Melbourne airport with nowhere to go and nothing but my panic.

I had someone's contact information at the bank, but I didn't have any Australian coins to make a call. And they probably wouldn't know where the driver was anyway. It was pre-cell phones.

Mark arrived about twenty minutes late. I was really glad to meet him but he took me on a harrowing ride through the city.

Australians, like the British, drive on the opposite side of the road from North Americans, which means the steering wheel and the control pedals are on the right side of the car rather than the left, where I expected them.

I was terrified! I was sitting on what I considered the "driver's side" of the car and had no steering wheel or brake. I felt I was about to be crushed at any moment as cars came at me from every strange angle.

And it turned out Mark had a broad New Zealand accent, which made it as hard for me to understand as the workers in the airport. The whole experience was exhausting and overwhelming.

Mark dropped me safely at my charming hotel, and I was able to relax temporarily.

When I figured out the time zones and called my parents in L.A., I didn't get much sympathy, but I did get a few chuckles and the soon-to-be-familiar refrain, "Well, you CHOSE to go halfway around the world. What did you expect?" I didn't have an answer to that aside from tears and exhaustion.

Once I got to work the next day, I found that there was one person I DID know – my acquaintance (and soon-to-be friend) Scotty from my former bank in L.A., who had also taken a job in Melbourne.

Men wore ties to work then, and he had his flipped over one shoulder as if he didn't have a care in the world. He hugged me and pretended not to notice the tears in my eyes. I was never so happy to see a familiar face in my life.

The next day, Scotty introduced me to a raft of "Yanks" who had been brought in for the project and a heap of Aussies whom I would soon call friends. I started to feel more at home.

Daily life was hard to get used to, though, as I had come from the land of twenty-four-hour grocery stores. In Melbourne, the stores were only open until six pm, and you couldn't buy meat after a particular hour due to some bizarre deal with the meat-cutters union and they were not open Saturday or Sunday. I very soon moved to a traditionally Jewish neighborhood, where shopping for anything on Saturdays was allowed. Driving on the other side of the road left me drained for about three months.

Other things along the way reminded me that I was an outsider. I arrived in Australia in August, which is winter in the southern hemisphere. Because their winters are mild, it was common not to have central heating. There were wall heaters in the living room, but one was expected to have warm blankets in the bedroom.

When my cute new duvet (or doona, as they are called down under) wasn't cutting it, I went to the department store to buy an electric blanket. I was looking for the North American kind where the electric blanket goes over the sheet and under the quilt.

The salesperson kept telling me these things did not exist in Australia, and I kept insisting they must, getting angrier. Suddenly, I was surprised and annoyed to be in tears once again.

I've dissected this incident repeatedly because it was so odd. I think my anger was because I set out to do something easy, something I expected would be the same in any language, something for my self-care, and it turned into an ordeal.

There are so many silent stressors when you move somewhere new that my stress was suddenly in my face—tears, and anger, rather than in the quiet background where I wanted them to be, were on display.

In case you would think that my early, frustrating experiences colored my entire two-year stay, they didn't. I eventually made peace with the differences and made some treasured friends.

I no longer expect significant changes to be easy, however, so I am less likely to jump in without thinking. I am more aware of my reaction to change now.

I can try to soften the impact by not piling on too much at once, making a list of possible outcomes, preparing, and giving myself space to decompress.

I MEET "THE ONE"

> "Courage doesn't happen when you have all the answers. It happens when you are ready to face the questions you have been avoiding your whole life."
> -Shannon Alder

I got married when I was thirty-nine.

You've heard stories about being set in your ways after a certain point in life, and that was very true of me. I had been single and lived alone for much of that time.

One of the most unexpected ways that fear hit me was when I first started dating Mike, who is my husband now.

In a previous chapter, I talked about how my father died when I was five.

I didn't realize until I fell in love with Mike that my father dying affected me as if he had abandoned us. And it had colored all my relationships, including this one, with that belief.

In hindsight, I can see that my relationships before Mike were with people I could love but would not have to commit to. Some I had started dating because they were interested in me rather than me being interested in them. It was flattering but unsustainable.

Of the men I had been interested in, there were often fundamental differences in family dynamics, priorities, values, and essential compatibility.

For instance, I dated a man whose mother was bipolar. His family life growing up was unpredictable. His mother married and divorced several times due to her illness. He was very uncomfortable with the closeness and predictability that a family like I was raised in developed over the years. The kind of family I continued to want. I always felt like I was trying to bridge the gap with both sides to no avail.

With the help of sound therapists, I eventually realized that I was sabotaging my desire to be in a sustainable love relationship through my choices.

It was as if my subconscious thought that if they were all going to leave/abandon me anyway, then why pick one I could love the way I wanted to be loved and fit into my family life? I could leave them without an existential crisis when things inevitably didn't work out.

Mike was in a fundamentally different category, which I discovered by way of the irrational fears I developed concerning our relationship.

You, see, I was sure Mike was dead if he was more than five minutes late meeting me or calling. I wasn't just worried that he was hurt or wouldn't show up for some other reason. I was obsessed with the idea that he would die and I would never see him again.

The argument that he was unlikely dead didn't lessen the fear, which was excruciating. I looked up the word excruciating to ensure I was using it properly, and I am.

Excruciating (adj): (1) Intensely painful. (2) mentally agonizing; very embarrassing, awkward, or tedious

Intensely painful. My stomach would tighten into a painful knot. I would feel frantic in that "fight or flight" as my heart beat too loud and too hard. I would cry and pace around. Neither Mike nor I (or my closest friend, for that matter) understood why I thought he was dead.

So the second definition was also true (embarrassment, awkward, agonizing). I have never been so confident and devastated by a circumstance with many other possible explanations. Mike could have been caught in:

Unexpected traffic.
A phone call or conversation that ran long.
A work emergency.
Extended dinner with the kids.
Or a last-minute errand, like gassing up the car.

This was long before cell phones with emails and texting in your pocket, so there weren't convenient ways to be in touch.

If you were out and about and running late, you would need to find a pay phone, get out of the car, get some change, then place your call. It was easy to think you might as well hurry on to your destination. Because who would possibly think you were dead every time?

The fear of abandonment was extreme. I tried to manage it by not talking about it and keeping my head together, but I had to find a better way.

I don't know how I did it, but it got easier. Over time I convinced my subconscious, the part that isn't open to logical thinking, that Mike wouldn't go away. Thankfully, now I only get *annoyed* when he's not adhering to my schedule.

And there was another big thing I wasn't prepared for.

About a year after I got involved with Mike, I met his three kids. It was the year before we married, so I was thirty-eight, and they were seven-twelve. I had made it through the "Mike's dead" phase, so I was pretty sure I was ready for whatever life would hand me after that.

Another company bought Mike's employer and my consulting gig ended, so we decided to leave Arizona and go to California to work together. The kids were young and had been through a lot with the divorce and their dad leaving town, so we decided to wait before introducing me to them.

I began to understand how gut-wrenching it was for Mike not to be closer to the kids when his weekends with them left him spent and sad, regardless of whether he was visiting them in Arizona, or they were visiting him in California.

I had a great role model for how to be a stepparent. Doug, the man I call Dad, was my mom's high school sweetheart, and they married when I was ten.

He had moved to the US for college and had kids in California from his first marriage. He had recently moved to Salt Lake City, Utah, and he seemed to step into our lives easily. Or rather, we stepped into his life since we moved from Montreal to Salt Lake City so we could all be together.

I can't remember any times when he insisted on his way instead of my mom's, and he brought a lot of new experiences into our lives.

I remember that I liked to put my hand in his hand when we were in a crowd of adults as if to say, "See this guy? He's my dad now."

None of us were saintly – there were plenty of disagreements and emotional times, especially when I was a teenager. But for the most part, being a stepparent "seemed" easy. I figured if he could do it so smoothly and successfully, so could I.

When our kids came for the summer, I didn't count on how accustomed I was to quiet and having my way. My dad became a stepparent in his early thirties and had been living with four kids of his own. I was thirty-eight years old and had lived alone for eight years. In my house, my stuff was my stuff, and it didn't get moved or used by anyone else.

Compare that to a place with three young, active kids and usually a friend or two. They were excited to see their dad for a couple of days but it was two days in a strange house and city. They believed, as most kids do, that everything in dad's house was also theirs. It had always been that way, so why wouldn't it be now?

The kids were kids. And my reaction was shock and panic!

I had paid attention to all the wrong things. I decorated their bathroom with brightly colored towels in baskets and cute art on the walls as if it were a guest bathroom when what they really needed were towel racks and more washcloths.

I had this little territorialism about my home. I was upset when no one cared to keep the towels, which were discolored by acne medication, folded neatly in the basket. This made me feel apprehensive: would I no longer have any control over my environment?

And the kids were curious about their dad's new life. They wanted to know what rules were different here. For instance, at our house, they could watch cable TV. What stuff did I have in my makeup drawer that they could try on?

What is life here on the weekends and in the summer going to be like? How can we get more of Dad's attention?

I was unprepared for living with three active kids in the beginning. I was relieved to head to work every morning because I knew what to expect there. My days were not predictable but they were somewhat somewhat orderly, and I didn't feel like an old, single, childless fish out of water. I was unfamiliar with my new home life, but I knew how work *worked*. Whew.

Most of the time at home, I felt like someone to be endured rather than a bonus adult, like I had felt with my stepdad.

Like with the "Mike is Dead" phase, time was my friend. I was determined not to give up on my life with Mike just because I felt uncomfortable and immature in this situation.

So I put one foot in front of the other every day, reminding myself why I had chosen to do it. Reminding myself of the stakes should I give up. Reminding myself that I was courageous, that the kids would adjust, that I would adapt, and that, to my delight and astonishment, Mike would help take care of me when I needed it.

COURAGE RISES

NOW CANCER?

"Courage is making the leap when you must – not when you're ready."
-Ashish Goel

In 1999, Mike and I moved back to Phoenix from Los Angeles for work. Mike's ex took the younger two kids to North Carolina to be closer to her family, but we had our oldest with us. We were settling in and working it out.

I tried to remember to do breast self-exams every so often because of my family history of cancer. I only did it about three times a year. I figured that was better than no times a year, right?

One night in April, as I was lying next to Mike, trying to drift off to sleep, I remembered to do it. I had always wondered if I would recognize a bad lump if I felt it because my breasts had always been dense and lumpy (cystic, they call it).

I didn't like what I felt. I knew the lump under my fingers had not been there the last time I did the self-exam, and it was hard, not pliable.

Agh! Danger! My heart leapt into my throat. What should I do?

After calming myself down with thoughts like "don't panic - you've always had some lumps and bumps" and "it's probably nothing," I decided to do the rational thing – ignore it for a few days and see if it would go away. Thumbs up, winky-face.

After those few days, I tried again. The lump was hard to find since it was close to the chest wall. Yep – still there, still hard. I would need to do something now.

I told Mike about it, and he was supportive but also optimistic. Plenty of people have lumps that turn out to be nothing. One of my sisters had one. I was pretty young for it to be cancer so let's not jump to conclusions.

I went to my gynecologist, and she validated that we should take a closer look at it.

My doctor ordered a mammogram, an ultrasound, and a core-needle biopsy. The core needle is hollow, and it has a spring. When activated, it plunges into the tumor (that's what we were calling it by now) and grabs a sample of it for analysis.

Because the tumor was so close to the chest wall, the needle accidentally nicked the bone, which was very painful. That was the most pain I felt during the entire experience.

After the biopsy, we waited for what seemed like *forever* to get the results. I was a wreck because I was convinced it was malignant. Due to my father's death from cancer when I was young, I had previously thought it was a matter of *when*, not *if*, I would get it.

My brain went into overdrive. Why was it taking so long? How long do lab tests take anyway? Surely not this long. It must be complex and lethal, a particular cancer they don't know how to treat. I'm sure it's terrible news.

Were they figuring out how to tell me I only had a week/month/year to live? At the same time, I didn't want to seem like a baby (get a grip!) I kept most of those dismal thoughts to myself.

After about ten days, my gynecologist's office called and asked me to come in for the results. This can't be good, I thought. Why not tell me over the phone that everything was fine?

At this point, I was confident that the tumor was malignant and steeled myself for the meeting with my doctor. Mike came with me, just in case. It was two days after my forty-third birthday.

When she delivered the news I had been expecting, I went a little numb. She outlined what should happen next – find a surgeon and an oncologist and make a plan.

She gave me paperwork about hormones and growth rates that I didn't understand because I didn't hear a word she said after "cancer." Mike was dumbstruck.

I called my closest friends and my family. My best friend, Sandee, showed up immediately. Debi, a two-time cancer survivor, came with a dozen pink roses an hour later.

There were tears and fears, and phone calls were returned after messages were left. There was also the weird phenomenon whereby the person with cancer consoles the person they are calling as that person hears the news for the first time. Many of my survivor friends have mentioned this.

That was ok with me, though, because my numbness morphed into a sense of certainty. I would be okay.

It was a physical sensation that I was laying down with my cheek on the hand of the infinite and holy, which I call God (feels and smells like rose petals, BTW), and she made me understand that I was going to be sticking around on earth for a while yet.

I've never had an experience like that before or since, but I was grateful for it. And it made telling the news easier.

Debi had great recommendations for a surgeon and an oncologist, so I saw them and enrolled them on my team.

I wanted the tumor out *yesterday,* but the surgeon said I needed to heal from the biopsy since I was still in pain. I didn't like this at all. Waiting sucks. I had already waited ten days for the biopsy results after the mammogram and the ultrasound. I did not want to wait anymore.

I was initially confident of the outcome, but every day we waited for surgery eroded that confidence; what if that one extra day was the day that one rogue cell would go on a Ms. Pac-Man spree through my bloodstream and other organs?

I didn't know then that the cancer had been growing long before being detected and that another week or two wouldn't affect the outcome. Even if someone had told me this, I'm not sure I would have listened then.

Surgery day finally came. I was getting a lumpectomy, and I was poked and prodded and felt up and shot up with nuclear stuff that would show my lymphatic pathways because they were taking the nodes, too.

When you have breast cancer, your breasts are not your own during treatment. Someone always wants to have a look, feel the scarring, push what you have left around, and say, "that's not bad." Yeah – not bad unless it's you.

Fast forward.

Surgery complete.

Clean margins were achieved.

Seventeen lymph nodes were removed.

I had to have more tumor testing and node testing.

Now my oncologist has the results. His diagnosis? "Stage 2B invasive ductal carcinoma with three lymph nodes that also showed cancer cells."

That meant chemo for me, but he came prepared. He was confident in the number of rounds of chemo (six—one every three weeks), and the number of rounds of radiation (thirty), and he knew when he wanted me to start.

Finally, I was going to *do* something instead of waiting. I'm sure I hugged him, but I might have kissed him, too.

Just because I was pretty confident of the outcome didn't mean I wasn't afraid. For the first few months, every time I started researching on the internet, I got nauseated and couldn't continue. If I wanted to know something, I had to ask Mike to look it up.

It was a primal, existential kind of fear. Cancer affects your family as well. Mike and I made an appointment with our favorite pastor at church to pray over my health, and it was the first and only time I had ever seen Mike cry. It broke my heart a little.

I started chemo at the beginning of June. It wasn't bad that first time. I felt terrible for a few days and was okay for the rest of the three weeks. A little tired but not as awful as I had expected from that kind of poison.

It started raining hair precisely fourteen days later. I cut off my long hair when I had the first chemo round in anticipation of the loss. My oncologist told me exactly when it would start, and he was right. Something about new follicles and bond formation in the hair being interrupted by the chemo: I walked out the front door and ran my hands through my hair, and the hair kept raining. No pain, no tugging, like when you run a comb or brush through your hair. Just lots of loose hair. And a lot of it was white – I had coincidentally stopped coloring my hair about four months before I had it cut. My natural color had grayed considerably, mainly in the front.

If the chemo had any role in leaving me with the primarily white crown I have now, I say a belated thank you. But it was time to shave it. I didn't like that I could grab a chunk of hair in the shower, and it would stay in my hand rather than on my head.

I am one of those women who loved being bald. I often wore a hat or scarf when I went out because people would look at me with pity in their eyes, and I didn't want that.

I was a warrior fighting for my life, and I would rather they see that than a poor, pitiful, bald girl.

My younger sister had her first child during this period, and we have a funny photo of my bald, bedazzled head next to her massive tummy. It still makes me laugh.

Even though I was confident I would live, the blood tests every three weeks before chemo worried me.

How would my white counts be?

How would my red counts be?

Were the results going to be good enough that I could proceed with the chemo?

I wanted to get it over with and not do the next round at the same time.

Over time, chemo affected me more and more. Round one was three bad and eighteen good days. By round six, it was nineteen bad days and two so-so days. I remember crying before the last round, begging Mike not to make me do it.

The chemo nurses were cheerful, attentive, informative, and full of great tips and recommendations. Once we got to know each other better, one of them told me they called Mike "Newspaper Man" because he came with me to every chemo session and brought all the reading that he had not had time to get done.

I was allergic to one of the chemo compounds – it gave me hives – so they would pump me full of Benadryl before they gave it to me. I tried to read but mostly dozed through the hours-long infusion sessions.

I had a break between my last round of chemo in November 2002 and my first round of radiation in January 2003.

For the radiation, they brought me in for measuring and tattooing to make lead blocks to ensure that they only hit the affected parts of my breast when the radiation was delivered. The small black dot tattoos helped the techs line up the blocks.

I used to notice the tattoos every time I looked bare-chested in the mirror, but they have faded and are harder to find.

Radiation was daily, every weekday, for ten minutes over six weeks. It made me tired but not sick, so that was a bonus.

I was so glad to be done with it all in February.

When it was over except for a daily pill, all I could do was trust the process. We had all done our part to work the project plan, and the project was over.

I had some souvenirs - a lingering but temporary metallic taste in my mouth from the chemo, a bald head, a pretty nifty scar, a few tattoo dots, brain fog (aka 'chemo brain'), and early menopause.

I was somewhat comforted by the stats that showed that the vast majority (85%) of people with my type and stage of cancer were cured by the treatment I had just completed.

I saw my oncologist every three months in the beginning. That gradually became every six months and then once a year.

I saw him again at the five-year mark and was prepared to celebrate. Then he told me my survival odds had only increased by 5%.

I was expecting the odds of survival to jump to 98%, and I became fearful all over again. A 10% chance of recurrence seemed like a lot to me after what I had already been through.

I started thinking about what I would do if it came back. Did I have another chemo fight in me? I decided I did but maybe only one. Of course, a recurrence or metastasis would lower my chances of survival.

Now I was worried about that. I was down for a couple of weeks. I gradually decided I had done all I could and just had to stick it out. I had a great life outside of cancer and learned much about myself and others.

I intentionally put it out of my mind as much as possible, and eventually, the fear faded. I had a few scares between then and now but learned not to jump to the worst-case scenario until all the evidence was in. They turned out to be nothing to worry about.

I have been cancer free for twenty-one years this year, and the odds of my survival are approaching those of a person that never had breast cancer.

There aren't adequate words to describe my gratitude. I learned to live life fully because we are not guaranteed years, months, or even days with loved ones.

THE THING THAT SCARES ME THE MOST

> "It's a courageous act to just be with what's happening at the moment - all of it, the difficult as well as the wonderful."
> —Eileen Fisher

My mom died of Alzheimer's disease.

In an earlier chapter, we looked at the definition of fear: An unpleasant, often strong emotion caused by anticipation or awareness of danger. If anyone embodied this definition with the expectation of trouble, it was me.

The Alzheimer's genes live in my family. My grandmother, my uncle, and her only daughter, my mom, had it. There were probably more instances, but I wasn't aware of them.

From 1997 through 2019, I watched my mom suffer and slowly die of Alzheimer's.

She had been intelligent, funny, decisive, creative, and present. Regardless of the times we butted heads or disagreed, I could make her laugh until the last couple of years when she was medicated so she wouldn't strike out at the kind staff in the memory care unit where she lived.

We knew she had memory deficits, but I didn't realize how bad it had become. I had seen her at home, still driving to familiar places and able to take care of her household.

Around 2004, when I owned a mosaic art supply business, mom came down to visit us in Arizona on her own. She was living in the Vancouver, BC, area at the time.

I had previously agreed to tag along on a two-day business trip with a friend to the Seattle area, leaving the day before Mom was to go home to Canada.

I locked up the store and gave mom the keys to my car and directions to a quilt shop she wanted to visit.

I figured Sky Harbor airport was unnecessarily complicated for her to navigate, so I took a taxi to the airport. When I got there, I realized I didn't have my wallet and figured it must have fallen out in my car when I drove to work that morning.

Knowing mom would be home by now, I took a taxi back to the house, but there was no car and no mom. We had practiced the route from the shop to the house several times, and I had left her a map and written directions on the car's front seat, but I started to worry that she had gotten lost.

I had given mom my phone number and Mike's phone number with the map and directions in case she had any issues, and Mike was going to take her out to
dinner after he got home from work. Everyone was clear on the plan.

I called Mike, but no word from mom. I called my dad in Vancouver to see if she had called him when she got mixed up. No dice there, either.

Both of them were ready now, in case mom did call. If she called Dad, he was going to call Mike to go pick her up. And Mike was prepared, so I grabbed an alternate ID and headed back to the airport.

I kept checking my phone messages until the plane took off, but no word from her. We landed in Portland, Oregon, and I rechecked my messages and called Dad and Mike. No word from mom.

By now, I was in tears. What kind of a daughter leaves her brain-damaged mom to fend for herself in a strange city? A bad one, I was sure.

Our plane completed the last leg to Seattle. Rechecking messages, I found that mom had left me a phone message five minutes earlier, saying she was at the Target store near my house and didn't know how to turn off my car alarm and asked if I could come and pick her up. She sounded beyond exhausted.

I can only imagine the journey she had made over several hours, trying to figure out where she was and where she should be going. The fact that she made her way within three miles of my house was astounding! She must have arrived at some clarity to get her there.

Mike went to pick her up at Target, and she went straight to bed because she was exhausted from the day. I felt like the worst daughter in the world.

I didn't know she wouldn't be able to handle that outing. She had "cleaned up" the map and notes I had left her by putting them out of her sight in the back seat, where she didn't remember to look for them when she got turned around. She forgot the map, the instructions, the phone numbers, and our practice runs in the car until she found them more than three hours after she had set out from the shop.

The whole experience blew my mind. Especially how mom could fool us, and herself, that she was competent and not in danger.

Later, there was a time when mom was still living at home when my dad fell off the roof.

He was eighty. With a broken clavicle and ribs, Mom couldn't care for him. She could no longer find the silverware, let alone prepare a meal.

My sister lived in the same city. Lin is a veterinarian and has to work during the day. She couldn't assist with daytime care except on her days off. Lin was already spending every day off with mom, taking her to lunch and, running errands, getting her out of the house.

Since I could work from anywhere with good Wi-Fi, I flew to Idaho and set up an office in their spare bedroom. That way, I could help with meals, help Dad with his pain and meds, and hang out with them in the evenings.

I learned then that mom was much more capable in her own home. I then committed to spending time at home with her every four to six weeks, where she was much more present, comfortable, and less stressed. It was a privilege to be able to do that until she died.

I will never forget the last time I made her laugh. She was weak, and we had moved her into memory care after a short stay in the hospital because of a violent flu.

It seemed the most appropriate time to transition her to a care home. She wanted to leave with us at the end of the visit. We told her she was still in the hospital because she had been sick and weak. The weakness was real, so she didn't fight it too much.

One day when I was visiting, there was a visiting musician, a guitar player/singer. The music made mom smile, and she clapped her hands out of time with the music, so I asked her if she wanted to dance.

She made an effort to stand up, and I helped her. When the guitar music was playing, and we were dancing (more like swaying out of time with the music), I had to grab her by the belt on her pants to ensure she didn't fall. We smiled and hummed, and I made some silly gestures, and she laughed with me. It was not a common occurrence anymore, so I took a selfie of the two of us to remember it.

She thought it was funny that her face was on my phone.

As time passed, she became tired and frustrated at being in a place she didn't recognize and didn't want to be, and her medications were increased, so she wouldn't kick and otherwise lash out at the nurses and aides.

Mom stopped smiling and laughing as the disease progressed. She became non-verbal. She always remembered that we (me, Dad, my sisters) were part of her pack until the end.

She would recognize us when we came to visit. At first, she would wave and get out of her chair, asking us to take her home, and eventually, she would only raise her eyebrows in our direction.

That was reassuring but so sad. Mom couldn't have a conversation with me, and by the time I felt I was finally ready to talk about some of the things that bothered me about my family relationships when I was young, I couldn't speak to her about anything.

I watched as it stripped her of everything that made her my mom. I like to say her name aloud, hoping she will "hear" me and know she will never be forgotten. Mom/Christine/Chris/Mrs. Lobb.

These and other experiences with mom led me to be terrified of the disease.

I had found my soulmate, and we married when I was thirty-nine. We were building a beautiful and loving life together when Mom's symptoms began to show. She was right around the age I am now (early/mid-sixties) when she was diagnosed with cognitive impairment and memory issues. ALZ can only be diagnosed via autopsy, so they didn't give it that label as far as I know.

As it progressed, especially after we experienced the driving incident, I became obsessed with the thought that I would be next.

I had mom's congenital bunions.

I looked and sounded like her and occasionally forgot words or my train of thought in mid-sentence.

What other proof did I need?

I read about some studies that linked learning new things and doing particular puzzles with slowing the progression of the disease, so I became obsessed with doing some of those every day. I installed Lumosity in my life, brain puzzles you can do on your computer.

I've been computer literate since high school, so I didn't have any aversion to technology and thought the puzzles were fun, except for the numerical set theory ones. I had trouble with those, too. Another nail in the coffin, I thought, until I remembered that I hated those in high school, too. Phew.

I talked about Alzheimer's all the time; "When I lose my mind" was a common phrase I used.

Every day there was seemingly more evidence, which was a constant in my thoughts and actions. This worrying continued for years because I had a front-row seat to Mom's increasingly diminished state.

I had not yet heard the phrase "worrying is nothing but praying for a bad outcome," but I'm not sure it would have made a difference. How do you stop an obsessive fear?

My friends would say, "you're no worse than me," and "oh, that's normal for our age," but I didn't believe them. Couldn't they see that mom and I were carbon copies of each other? Didn't they know we liked the same activities and had matching but opposite-side back issues? I was sure that our similarities were a death sentence.

After a few years of this, I couldn't stand it. The costs were getting too great. I was worried

ALL the time. It was taking up too much room in my thoughts, crowding out other things, and I talked about it incessantly. I could never do enough of the unique puzzles on some days, even getting caught up in them during my workday. It made me sad and weary. It was bugging my friends (eye-rolling, subject changes, trying to convince me I was wrong.)

I eventually had to weigh the options: live in fear or face it head-on. Being a Take-Charge person, I decided to DO SOMETHING about it. Get my arms around MY version of the disease instead of guessing.

I learned that there was a thing called cognitive testing, which tests your memory, comprehension, and reasoning in about ninety different ways.

So I looked for hard evidence that my brain was the mess I knew it to be so we could plan for the best possible outcome.

In 2012, I discovered that a psychologist near my workplace did this testing, so I made an appointment.

Many individual tests are part of the comprehensive testing and it takes a few hours to get through. Some are with words, some with numbers, some require reading, and some require listening and repeating back. And set theory - my favorite.

It was a tiring afternoon.

It turns out, however, that the hard evidence I found was the opposite of my expectations. The doctor told me that I was on the high end of the typical spectrum for my gender and age, that I should be delighted with my capabilities, and that we would call that test a baseline.

If I perceive cognitive deficits in the future, I should come back, and we will compare. I started to listen more closely to my friends who said, "oh, that happens to me, too." They weren't freaking out about losing themselves.

I still had the fear and continued to worry, only marginally alleviated by the "normal" diagnosis. I did share my fear with others a little less because they kept reminding me I was "normal." I took the tests for a second time six years later.

I found the testing even more difficult because I second-guessed my results after each test and was sure I was not "winning." Sometimes knowing more about an upcoming trial is not a gift. It's torture.

What finally quieted my self-diagnosing, though, was the results of this second test. I did better than the first time I took it. What??

I didn't see that coming. And this time it *was* a relief.

But since this disease is entirely unpredictable and unknowable ahead of time, Mike and I decided to make some plans.

We've had discussions about the end of life. We have a trust set up and medical powers of attorney, and he knows that at the first sign of incompetency, I want us to move into a place for seniors with an active living section and a memory care section. That way, I could get used to the grounds and the setup, making it as familiar as possible, and move into the memory care unit when the time came. He would be on the property, making visits easy. We would never have to move again. We bought and fully paid for long-term care insurance while we still had our corporate incomes to offset the costs of care in case we needed it.

I keep my eye on the death with dignity movement. He knows that, after watching my mom lose the essence of herself and then waste away, I will prefer to die on my terms if I get the disease and there is no cure in sight.

In the US, the Right to Die is law in ten states currently, but ALZ is an exception because typically, an ALZ patient will not be able to make their own decisions within six months of their death.

However, it is legal, with caveats, in Switzerland. He seems very uncomfortable with this, and I am doubtful he would implement that plan, but I still voice my wishes.

These plans, and the testing results, have all ensured that Alzheimer's is not included in every conversation I have anymore and plays only a bit part in the drama that is my life. The fear never entirely disappears, but I have learned a better way to live with it.

COURAGE RISES

RETIREMENT

> "To think is easy. To act is difficult. To act as one thinks is the most difficult."
> - Johann Wolfgang von Goethe

In April 2018, Mike and I had an offer in on our would-be retirement home, which had only one floor so we wouldn't have to worry about stairs as we aged.

It was Easter weekend, so we gave them extra time to respond to our offer.

Meanwhile, we have our vacation home in the mountains for sale. The mortgage has been upside down since we bought it in 2006 (we owed more than the house was worth).

Our realtor calls - the vacation home has sold at a great price, which means we are mortgage free!

Free from our vacation home mortgage AND free from our permanent home mortgage. We were not expecting that much of a windfall. Dang!

On Easter Sunday morning, Mike looks me in the eye and asks me a question. We have decent savings, and my corporate IT salary has been paying for the vacation home plus expenses for that home and the mortgage for our permanent home in Phoenix.

"What would you prefer to do?" he asks. "Go ahead with this new house? Or retire?" We couldn't do both.

Holy Crap! I hadn't thought it through.

Can I choose to retire?

Just like that?

I mean, I know it's not "just like that." It's been a lot of hard work for thirty-seven years. Retirement was still just a concept in my head.

And yet, it only took me ten minutes. After asking him three times if he was sure, "Retire" was my answer!

OMG, OMG, OMG!

I loved retiring. I didn't miss my corporate job because it had morphed into something I didn't like. My friends threw me a fab retirement party, which my dad, older sister, and her husband flew in to attend.

I turned off the alarm clock and said yes to every invitation to play and travel. We even bought a motorhome, and I had time to drive it on my own to Montana for our first trip to Glacier National Park!

Mike was still working, so he flew into Kalispell, and I picked him up. That led to many other motorhome trips with him and my friends. I exhausted myself over that first year. And then I started feeling restless.

There were a bunch of reasons for the restlessness. But mostly, my identity, my image of myself, had always been entwined with what I did for a living.

As a consultant, I used to laugh with my friends about how people saw our unglamorous jobs in a glamorous light. The international jet-setting consultants. A silly phrase, perhaps, but I still saw myself as that woman – using my skills and wits to make a success wherever I went at whatever I needed to do.

In some ways, I was constantly proving my worth via my work. But that was no more. Who was I now? What would I do to add more purpose and meaning to my life? More success?

I did have a "side gig."

I joined an MLM[1] company about a year before I retired, mainly for a discount. I loved their products and wanted more, but I hate to pay retail prices for anything, so I became an independent distributor.

I bought a lot of it (too much), and my friends and family held parties in which *they* got products at a discount, and it was fun. I even had a couple of people sign up under me, so I had a team of two.

---

[1] Multi-level Marketing. Look it up.

Pretty soon, though, I exhausted the goodwill and wallets of my friends and didn't have an excellent vision to help my team members succeed.

Then I thought, "perhaps if I made a real go of it, this would be something I could wrap my identity around now."

There was only one problem - how was I going to meet more potential customers and team members? I no longer went places where other people hung out (like work) on a consistent basis.

I started networking!

I went to MeetUp.com and searched for networking events in Scottsdale, Arizona. It was close to where I lived, and those Scottsdale people have money! I put on something cute and headed out to lunch with the Scottsdale chapter of SEVEN Networking.[2]

I'm an extrovert and get energy from being with others, so I had a blast. The people were friendly, and they did such disparate things.

---

[2] https://s-e-v-e-n.org

The founder, Karen, our chapter leader, was very personable and welcoming. I loved lunching with these men and women for an hour and a half every week, finding out what they did, having one-to-one conversations about our lives and our businesses, and doing business with some of them.

I presented at a few meetings and made a few sales, but after six months, I thought I would be *more* successful.

One of the members, Kenyatta Turner[3], offered a twelve-week program that focused on behavior, productivity, and mindset.

I was impressed and inspired by Kenyatta regularly at the meetings. She had great insights about business and shared them regularly with the group. When she opened her mouth, I listened.

She expanded her business weekly, and I wanted to learn what she knew. The program was starting in December, so I signed up. And found what I was looking for.

---

[3] https://freedomempireconsulting.org

The mastermind was powerful, my fellow students were engaging, and we all learned from each other and Kenyatta.

The mastermind principle is based on the writing and practices of Napoleon Hill[4], but it's straightforward. Two/three/four heads are better than one when learning and solving problems. We studied and implemented two books geared toward success in business *and* life. Change your mindset, change your life.

I enrolled in the mastermind several times to continue implementing the principles from the books and get feedback and help from the group. It gave me incredible energy! I was getting out of bed in the morning, eager to learn and get on with my business!

The third time through, I had to confront that I was *not* doing the things in my business that would make me successful, such as booking parties and asking people to join my team.

I measured my money-making activities weekly and wasn't doing them. I got to share my measurement score every week with the

---

[4] Napoleon Hill, *Think and Grow Rich*, The Ralston Society, 1937

group and I got a one or zero out of six *every week*. I slowly realized I was keeping myself busy but not engaged with the right things. It was hard showing up every week and admitting that.

Then things changed. In one of the exercises, she asked a series of questions, including "what makes you unique?" My list looked like this:

- I'm tall (5'11")
- I have lived in three countries
- I'm a stepmom
- I'm retired
- I have courage
- I don't have to work anymore
- I love to travel
- I have two sisters
- My mom has ALZ
- I married at thirty-nine
- I have an easy time making friends
- I'm sixty
- I have white hair

Here's where the evidence appeared – in the list of things I believe make me unique. We reviewed the list when Kenyatta and I had a private coaching session.

I already knew, from my Behavioral SuperPowers assessment, that I am innately a Take Charge/ Spontaneous/ Fast Paced Influencer. The evidence has shown up in my life over and over since I was a child.

I also read that we can find a sense of purpose when we can be in service to others. This felt right to me, as I had always loved teaching people things; tech things, life things, musical things, etc.

We started talking about ways I could integrate The Influencer in me with the list somehow. Could I use my behavioral strengths (who and what I am) to do something unique in service to others?

Then she asked me what I wanted to do in life. I had thought about that over the months and knew it wasn't selling widgets.

I built up my nerve and said it aloud for the first time; "I want to do what YOU do. I want to help people think differently and create the life they want by coaching them to intentionally exercise courage." She said, "Why don't you do that, then?"

Boom! It changed everything. This idea resonated with me in a deep way. After many conversations with Kenyatta and some continued introspection, I stopped my MLM business, named my business Courage Rises, and set out to learn how to be a coach like my mentor.

I started by interviewing people about their everyday stories of courage and bravery to show that a choice to move forward in the face of adversity is courageous.

Many interviewees told me they didn't have any option but to carry on when this or that happened, but they did. They could have crawled up in a ball and refused to re-engage with life, but they chose to move forward instead. And I am proud to know all of them!

The road to becoming a Life Coach, a Fear and Courage Expert, a certified Behavioral SuperPowers coach, and a best-selling author has not been simple.

I thought I would have to take the courses, do the things, and talk to the people, but I hadn't counted on the internal resistance.

As I strove to be something more, to build something of value from whole cloth with just my skills and my wits, I ran into my fear over and over.

It showed up as procrastination, TV binging, phone-game playing, overeating, general avoidance, and ignoring my studies.

My particular and fundamental fears boil down to an issue of personal worthiness. I wasn't offering widgets for sale anymore. I would be offering *myself* to the public.

Maybe you've had these thoughts before, here and there. I started getting a constant stream of them.

- Who am I that people would listen to what I have to say?
- Why would people pay me to coach them?
- No one is going to want to read my book.
- People told me I was smart all my life, but I don't think it's true. They were being nice to me.

- Remember [fill-in-the-blank incident] where I was wrong out loud and felt humiliated?
- It's too late, lady. You're too old to have a big dream of leaving a legacy. It is going to be like so many other projects – left unfinished.

What the hell?! It was as if someone else was inside my head berating me about stuff that wasn't true.

It surprised me, as well, that some of the people I'm close to don't understand why I am reinventing myself at my age and are a little angry that I'm doing it. So on top of the stuff I am piling on myself, I'm afraid I may lose some friends.

Ouch!

You'll read in the next chapter that the statements above are limiting beliefs and stories.

We all have some form of them; they have been with us since we were seven. In my case, that was a helluva long time ago. Who says that little girl gets to decide who I am and what I do now?

As a result of all this resistance, along with a significant slowdown in progress, I am starting to understand what people mean when they say success and fulfillment in life have more to do with how you are <u>BE</u>ing than what you are <u>DOing</u>.

Think about it. We can all do things (barring physical or developmental disabilities) like organize our desks, tell a story, or show someone how to do something.

But you can do any one of those things, or all of them, over the long term and not achieve success.

To be successful over a long time, we must BE intentional, dedicated, thoughtful, humble, trustworthy, confident, and live in unity with our values.

And I have had at least one person tell me the opposite of all those limiting beliefs/stories.

As I am working on believing in myself and who I am BEing, I choose to listen to those people instead of the internal seven-year-old who thinks she is keeping me safe from life-threatening change.

The people who know who I am NOW.

FIVE WAYS TO LEAN IN TO FEAR TO CREATE THE LIFE YOU WANT

Why have I told you these stories?

I want to show you that even though I feel I have lived courageously most of my life, fear is a normal part of it. All of the fears I've told you about are still with me. They don't magically go away once you have dealt with them once. They may stage a repeat attack given the proper physical and emotional circumstances.

I want to illustrate some trusted and reliable methods to cope with them in this chapter. That's what I mean by "leaning in" to fear.

COURAGE RISES

THE 3 ROOTS OF FEAR – LIMITING BELIEFS, STORIES, AND DELUSIONS

> "I am constantly amazed at how courageous, and radical, speaking the truth is."
> —Melissa Etheridge

Do you know that research shows the only fears we are born with are the fear of falling and loud noises?

You will see evidence of that if you're around babies. They "catch themselves" even while sleeping when they suddenly stretch out their arms like they are trying to fly or stop themselves from falling. And they may start to wail when presented with loud noises they are unfamiliar with.

Some people, like me, have never really lost the noise thing. I love noisy, boisterous parties, but I don't like loud, sharp noises at home. It took me quite a while to get used to our teenagers slamming doors, as ours often did.

We gradually learn to overcome those fears with repeated noise exposure and feel safe with our caregivers.

The rest of our fears are learned over time based on our environment and experiences.

Home life, teachers, friends, bosses, bullies, the news, and things we observe or hear lead us to form emotional opinions about what we see or feel. Those passionate opinions can lead us to limiting beliefs, stories, and delusions.

Limiting beliefs are beliefs that prevent us from pursuing our goals and desires. They keep us from doing important things, like applying for a dream job or finding the relationships we want (or leaving the ones we don't want).

They are thoughts and opinions that we believe to be the truth. They tend to negatively impact our lives by stopping us from moving forward and growing on a personal and professional level.

Some examples are,
- I'm fat.
- I'm too tall.
- I'm dumb.
- I'll never be thin.
- Men leave.
- I'm undesirable.
- I'm damaged.

Can you guess what percentage of your limiting beliefs formed when we were seven? Ninety percent. Nine-zero.

That's crazy!

I remember being seven. That is no time for you to form *rational* opinions about yourself, who or what you are or aren't.

Stories are the stories you may have grown up with that people told you about yourself or YOU told yourself based on your experiences, and they can be just as limiting.

You may have formed these stories in moments of stress/humiliation/crisis and integrated them into who you believe yourself to be.

Examples:
- I'll never be good enough to play (music, sports, or video games) professionally.
- I don't know how to make new friends so I won't make any friends in my new school.
- I'm ugly [or fat, or tall, or dumb, or freckled, or differently-abled], so no one will want to go out with me.
- I'll never make any money at that.

These stories come at us from so many different directions. Many times, they are the result of someone else's stories to *themselves* that they are repeating out loud. They make us fearful that something we want will be forever unattainable.

Delusions are a little different because they can have a kernel of truth.

- I'm not tall (true), so I can't play basketball (not true).
- This person knows more than I do (perhaps), so I could never do what they do (nope)
- They already have a mom (true) – they won't ever want a relationship with me (not true)

With delusions, we equate that one part of the thought is genuine, with the other part being true, even though they may not have anything to do with each other.

For instance, Isaiah Thomas, who plays for the Charlotte Hornets professional basketball team, is not a tall guy. He is an average height for a man from the USA at five feet nine inches. And yet Isaiah is an NBA All-Star multiple times.

If someone had implanted that delusion that he was not tall enough to play basketball professionally in his head when he was young, he would not be a household name today (if you live in a basketball household, that is).

Surfer Bethany Hamilton had her arm torn off by a shark while surfing when she was thirteen. She could have turned that into a delusion that, because she lost her arm, she would never surf professionally, care for kids, or do any of the many amazing things she does today.

These limiting beliefs, stories, and delusional thoughts (and they are just that – thoughts you choose to have) will limit your actions toward your brave goals for more and better.

Let's look at how.

THE FEAR CYCLE

> "Life shrinks or expands in proportion to one's courage."
> - Anaïs Nin

Coach and best-selling author Katie Draznin illustrates the Fear Cycle this way[5]:

---

[5] Katie Draznin, Tell Fear You're The Boss, (Amazon, 2021)

Fear Cycle

In this model,

- Fear causes inaction.
  For instance, Angela's fear of being judged may lead her not to speak up about her idea at work.

- Inaction makes you have a LESSER Experience in Life.
  Because Angela doesn't speak up, her view isn't heard. Someone else brings up the idea, maybe even the same one, and gets a coveted assignment/project.

- Lesser Experience means you will have LESSER ABILITY in life.

Because she didn't speak up, she didn't learn the lessons or have exposure to new people, thinking, and processes that the assignment or project would present.

- Which causes more fear.
  Angela may now be afraid that others are learning faster than she is, and she isn't keeping up, which leads her to repeat the cycle.

Or John has moved to a new town and wants to have friends, but he hasn't had to make new friends in years. He wants to skip right to the part where the routines and understandings of old friends exist without trying.

He intends to *have* friends without having to *make* friends.

His fear of not being attractive enough or worth befriending keeps him from accepting invitations or going to events to meet people.

Because he doesn't flex this meet-and-greet muscle, he doesn't build confidence in his ability to make friends, which keeps him stuck with few to no friends, day after day, week after week, and maybe even a year.

You can see how these two examples not only maintain the status quo of inaction but manage to pile additional fears onto the originals. Pile on too many worries, and you will be crushed under their weight.

Why It's Important to Break the Cycle

The relative anonymity of social media makes it easy for people to criticize and pass judgment on others without being truthful, fair, or facing the judged. No one needs to take feedback from people who are not brave in their own lives; however, it doesn't remove the sting. And it doesn't stop our subconscious brains from adding to the limiting beliefs, stories, and delusions we have already formed.

Time is a non-renewable resource. We can't get it back if we don't use it to build what we want in life - joy, meaning, purpose, impact, legacy, money, [your dream here].

Why spend that time making yourself and your life small because you are afraid to make it bigger, better, or more? And if my retirement story has anything to teach, it's that it is never too late to create the life you have dreamed of.

COURAGE RISES

METHODS FOR MOVING THROUGH FEARS

> "Give credit to yourself. Celebrate your wins. Allow the word courage to integrate into your thoughts about you."

My experience and research have led me to five effective methods for confronting fear so you can move through it. I'll lay them out here and relate them to the stories you read earlier in this book.

Get Clear on Your Motivators

A motivator provides a reason or stimulus to do something. One of the big motivators in my retirement years is my dream house.

I'll call it my Love Mansion.

My happiest place is where my family and friends can gather, celebrate, and love on each other. And I want to supply the venue.

I love it when we have a crowd of loving friends and family around eating, playing, laughing, and even crying together, so I want a large house in a beautiful location that can sleep at least twelve people.

I want to host parties and provide a place where people will want to hang out.

I have tried to quit my plans for a big, beautiful, meaningful life in retirement many times because of fear, which sounded like

- "I don't know how to build it."
- "It'll be hard."
- "I could never afford that because I don't make money anymore."

as well as other limiting thoughts and beliefs.

When I looked at why I stopped moving forward, I decided I wasn't ready to give up my

Love Mansion as a dream and a reality. I would figure out how to build it. I would put in the hours to read and learn and do and BE so that I *could* afford it.

What motivates you to do things you wouldn't otherwise do? Who or what do you do something for?

If it's you, that's completely legit! Your happiness and fulfillment are every bit as important as anyone else's. Moreso, in most cases.

Make a list of your motivators and refer to it when fear stops you.

I have a friend who is motivated by giving her grandchildren incredible experiences in life. I have another who is motivated to make an impact in her community by helping to make the lives of the homeless less bleak. I'm motivated to be healthier for my twin grandsons. Skiing is a joyful activity in my life, and I want to be a skiing grandma well into my seventies.

Weigh The Options

The Pro/Con list. You have probably heard of this simple exercise but never connected it to fear.

But why wouldn't you make a difficult decision if you weren't afraid to make the wrong one? Here's a straightforward example.

I'm scared of spiders—huge ugly ones.

In Australia, they have spiders called huntsmen. They are big and hairy, like a tarantula in the USA but with smaller bodies and longer legs. They're one of the few things in Oz that won't kill you, but that doesn't make them any less terrifying.

One night I'm in my apartment bedroom, and I've taken off my glasses and some movement catches my eye on the ceiling, so I look up. Over in the corner of the room, near my closet, was a dark smudge on the ceiling. I'm pretty sure it's a spider, but I don't have my glasses on, so I'm not sure. Maybe it's just a moth or a watermark I never noticed before.

What to do?

Here's my options list:

Put on Glasses/Look	Go To Sleep
I would have to do something with it if it's a spider	If it's a spider, it could move in the night, then I wouldn't know where it is
	Maybe it will crawl into my bed while I'm sleeping
	I would not be able to sleep knowing it's there

I don't know what you would do, but I put on my glasses. The Go To Sleep option had too many unacceptable outcomes.

It was a huntsman spider, so I prepared to do something with it that night, and hilarity (and more fear) ensued.

That's a story for another time.

I know this is a reasonably inconsequential story about an ugly spider, but what is your "ugly spider"?

Are you an introvert who gets invited to a party?

Have you been offered a new job in a new company? In Australia?

Maybe you are trying to decide whether to invest in yourself through a course or a seminar.

Make your lists.

What will the thing cost you in terms of money, time, skills, comfort, self-esteem, and peace of mind? What will not doing something cost you?

Just Jump In!

I used this method in my decision to go to Australia. Since I had been thinking, "if not now, then *when*," I chose NOW and jumped in.

I had been telling myself I was brave since I was twenty-three, so this decision fit my view of myself. I figured out how to live, shop, work, and play once I got there.

Just Jump In doesn't mean there will be no fear; you simply have faith that everything in your lie is figureoutable.[6] That you will

---
[6] Phrased coined by Marie Forleo in her book *Everything Is*

overcome the specific fear bridges when they present themselves.

This is an intuitive manner of dealing with fear, and it's not for every situation.

How do you feel about your ability to figure things out? What areas of your life are you ready to stop dithering over and just jump in?

Name Your Fear

Create a relationship with your fear as if it were a person. I love this method because it can help to neutralize the internal feelings of dread that sometimes come with fear.

So – what? – name it Fred or Barb?

Yes – it can be that simple.

Many people name their fear after a creature or a person that made them afraid or feel small in the past.

I know of a person who called her fear Boo Radley, after the shadowy neighbor in the novel *To Kill a Mockingbird*. Perhaps you will

---

Figureoutable, (Portfolio, 2019)

name yours after a former teacher or a family member; Grandpa, Grandma, Dad, or Mom.

Once you name your fear, you can take it out of your head, sit it down, and talk to it. Close your eyes and pretend you are looking at Boo, Ms. Johnson, or Mom.

Acknowledge your fear and start a dialogue. Mine usually start with, "you are pissing me off right now because I want to [fill in the blank], and you are holding me back."

Give this a try and see if you can diminish the physical effects of fear on you by envisioning it as someone.

Elizabeth Gilbert, who wrote the book *Eat, Pray, Love*, didn't name her fear, but she addressed it directly like this[7]:

---

[7] Elizabeth Gilbert, *Big Magic: Creative Living Beyond Fear,* Riverhead Books, 2015. Artistic rendition by April Hadley

> **FEAR**: "I recognize and respect that you are part of this family, and so I will never exclude you from our activities, but still—your suggestions will **NEVER** be followed. You're allowed to have a seat and you're allowed to have a voice, but you are not allowed to have a **VOTE**. You're not allowed to touch the road maps; you're not allowed to suggest detours; you're not allowed to fiddle with the temperature. **DUDE**, you're not even allowed to touch the radio. But, above all else, my **DEAR** old familiar friend, you are absolutely **FORBIDDEN** to drive." –Elizabeth Gilbert

What will you call *your* fear?

<u>Tell Fear You're the Boss</u>

There are many acronyms used for the word fear. Some examples are

- Fuck Everything and Run
- Frantic Efforts to Avoid Reality
- Future Events Appearing Real
- False Evidence Appearing Real

But I prefer the Fear Formula,[8] which looks like this:

I like it because it recognizes that fear is normal and we can do something about it.

- **Forgive** your fear because it's a normal part of life. It's your brain making you uncomfortable, but only so it can keep you safe from harm.

---

[8] Ibid. Draznin. © The Journey Within

- **Embrace** your fear. Lean in. Say hello. Thank it for trying to keep you safe. But tell it you've got this.

- **Act.** Taking action is about engaging your fear with the intent to move through it. The steps can be big or small. Some people are afraid to get out of bed, so their big, intentional act might be to stand up and put on their slippers. Others may do that easily but struggle with speaking up at work. Their big, deliberate action might be to raise their hand in a meeting and add to the dialogue.

  Action / movement can be challenging, but it can also build confidence. And remember – no one can tell you if an action is brave or big except you. If you feel it's big, it is! Use the tools in this chapter to engage.

- **Repeat** as necessary. As I said, you may move past specific fears in a moment or a season of your life only to have them return. Repeat this formula with new or old fears returning for a visit.

<u>Start Leaning In to Fear Today!</u>

Make a list of fears. Choose the one you want to push through, select one of the tools above, and start. Make a declaration that you're going to do it. Use this template:

The fear I want to move through is:

_____

_____

In the next [Pick one]: ___ 1 ___ 3 ___ 6 months, I am going to take the following action:

_____

_____

How many times? How frequently?

_____

Be realistic – you probably won't be able to solve your existential dread of climate change (for instance) by repeating an affirmation three times a day. Make the action suitable for the timeframe and the fear.

Got it? Now you can share it! **Tell two people.**

This is important. In my workshop, Tell Fear You're The Boss, we tell the whole class. Ask the people you tell to check in with you monthly/ weekly/whatever makes sense. This will remind you of your commitment to yourself if you slip into complacency and comfort instead of taking action. It will help you hold *yourself* accountable.

Why tell people? Because transformation is a public event, so declare your intentions out loud. It may inspire others to lean into *their* fears!

COURAGE RISES

ADDITIONAL RESOURCES

"You are braver than you believe, stronger than you seem, and smarter than you think."
-A. A. Milne

Congratulations on taking a step, investing in your growth, and leaning in!

Change can be challenging and slow, especially when fear gets in your way. You may wonder where you can get more help leaning into fear in your life.

Join my Courage Convergence to get a free list of clickable links to books and podcasts I like about fear, bravery, courage, and mindset.
https://couragerises.site/convergence

In addition you can have a free, no-obligation chat with me about how we might work together. Book a convenient time here.
https://couragerises.site/book-discovery

ABOUT THE AUTHOR

Suki (aka Susan) was born in Toronto, Ontario, Canada, and moved to the US at age 10 following her father's death and her mom's remarriage. After college, she spent 35+ years in Information Technology (IT) as a project/program manager and technical trainer where she developed keen insights and practices around people, communication, and leadership. After retiring from her tech career at 59, she got restless, believing she had more to give. She dove headfirst into personal development and, at 60, pivoted and started a new business and a purpose-driven life season.

She is now an international best-selling author, coach/mentor, courage expert, and is accredited in Behavioral Superpowers (she is a Spontaneous, Take-Charge Influencer) and Tell Fear You're The Boss coaching practices. She is also the host of a weekly inspiring live show on Facebook, LinkedIn and YouTube called Defying Expectations Over 60 (Tuesdays at 11 am Pacific Time).

A member of the Wisdom Generation (fka "seniors"), she is founder and Chief Empowerment Officer of Courage Rises, LLC. Suki helps women "Retire & Rewire" by helping them to clarify the vision of their future, understand their innate behaviors, build a positive relationship with fear, develop a growth mindset, and build the lives they want and deserve.

Suki is a wife, stepmom of three, and Grammy to twin boys. She is a serial entrepreneur, heart-centered leader, 20-year breast cancer survivor, world traveler, wine drinker, cactus-lover, and loving friend. She lives with her husband, Mike Jeffreys, in Phoenix, Arizona Connect with Suki on any of the following platforms:

Email: Suki@couragerises.life

Website: https://couragerises.life

Facebook: @susan.jeffreys, @couragerisespage

LinkedIn: https://www.linkedin.com/in/couragerises

Join the Courage Convergence and keep up with what's happening with Suki and Courage Rises. Join here:

https://couragerises.site/convergence?utm_medium=CRBook

Made in the USA
Middletown, DE
12 February 2023

23701646R00066